Flying Smart

Flying Smart

A Handy Guide
for the New Airline Traveller

Atul Bhatia

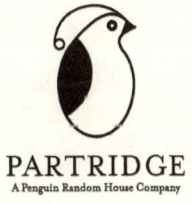

PARTRIDGE
A Penguin Random House Company

To order additional copies of this book, contact
Partridge India
000 800 10062 62
orders.india@partridgepublishing.com

www.partridgepublishing.com/india

Contents

Foreword

In 1975, I stood in my garden looking up as two MiG-21s from the nearby air base tore through the morning skies a mere 500 feet above my head. Days later, my father took me to the air base to meet the pilots and get to sit in the cockpit of that fighter. I was hooked!

A couple of years later, I took my first flight on an Indian Airlines Airbus A300. I think my decision to be a pilot was more or less made up by the time I got down that flight in Delhi.

Over the next four decades, as I graduated, earned my wings and flew Maritime Reconnaisance for the Indian Navy, I saw the Indian aviation industry evolve in fits and starts. We grew up in the socialist era, where one single nationalised airline held sway over the domestic market, while another flew globally. Years later, we saw the first wave of privatisation in the aviation sector, as myriad airlines rose to prominence, shone briefly, then faded out into oblivion. While the world aviation market was booming, India's aviation industry was languishing; in the days of 'Jai Jawan, Jai Kisan' and 'Garibi Hatao', the airline industry was considered a barely-tolerated niche segment for the millionaire traveller.

Captain Gopinath's bold decision to kickstart the stagnant industry with his low-cost carrier, Air Deccan in 2003 was the turning point. The very attractive pricing of tickets on his airline was a game changer as people turned away from the railways to this new, more glamorous and definitely faster way to travel. A slew of new airlines commenced operations in the next couple of years, and while their growth – and that of the industry – has been turbulent, civil aviation in India is definitely here to stay.

My own transition from the military to civil aviation happened in 2010 at which time the industry was still (yet again!) fairly nascent. Many of my friends were quite fascinated with aviation and I found myself answering many aviation-related questions or debating the finer points of air travel over many cups of coffee. Transitioning through various airports, I had the opportunity to learn about the aviation business in some detail and view its transformation through the eyes of our passengers and all our ground staff and other people who kept this well oiled machine running.

As I crisscrossed the country flying (many first time) passengers all over our vast country, my wife got her fair share of travel too. Her experiences and perspectives have provided some tremendously valuable inputs to this book. After all, she's flown as a passenger much more than I have!

CHAPTER I

So You Want to Fly

Indian commercial aviation is booming. Today, over 1500 flights are operated a day by five major airlines flying over 400 aircraft to destinations big and small all over the country. Flying has been transformed from a luxury service for the rich and famous, to an essential utility, with students, senior citizens, families on weekend breaks all taking to the skies. The explosion in air travel had the airlines, airports, regulators and the government all struggling to keep pace and ensure that safety and service standards are maintained. I'm glad to note though that the Industry has stabilised to a very large extent and the future of aviation in India is certainly rosy.

Contrary to popular opinion, travel by airlines is very, very safe. Stringent training standards, new aircraft, good infrastructure and regular, frequent audits by the Director General of Civil Aviation (DGCA), India's regulatory authority for civil aviation, all ensure that passenger safety is looked after.

Low-Cost vs Full Service

The launch of Deccan Aviation in 2003 heralded the arrival of Low Cost Carriers (LCCs) in Indian skies. The existing airlines of that time opted to continue as 'full service carriers', but a majority of the new entrants into the market chose the LCC route. So what really is the difference between the two?

Essentially, the difference boils down to services that are bundled with your ticket. The most visible bundled service is an option on seating. Full service carriers have First Class, Business Class, Premier Economy class (generally called by various imaginative names) over and above the regular Economy class. These classes offer varying degrees of personal space, personal service, better In-Flight Entertainment by way of larger screens and more channels, complimentary drinks, hot towels and newspapers and so on. All of this comes at a cost; a First Class ticket can be five times as expensive as a regular Economy class ticket.

Entry into this stratospheric club comes with a whole lot of other perks, such as valet services, access to lounges and spas at airports globally, frequent-flyer programs that allow the passenger to trade accumulated points for free flights or goodies, alliances that allow the passenger to fly on other airlines on the same ticket and so on.

For the cost-conscious economy class traveller, the complimentary meal served on board, and perhaps a frequent-flyer program is the only difference between a full service carrier and an LCC. The latter too works on the premise that you buy a ticket which is priced higher than the minimum-fare, non-refundable ticket offered to compete with encroaching LCCs.

LCCs on the other hand, tend to charge for every service, big or little, and future trends point to an increasing unbundling of services. You pay for booking your ticket online, you pay for a printout of the ticket if you've not already got it along with you. Some airlines charge for check-in baggage. Others charge for printing the boarding card if you did not use their web-check in services. A European LCC has been mulling the introduction of pay-to-use lavatories, while some LCCs have actually toyed with the idea of standing-room-only flights.

In the final analysis, which carrier you fly is dictated by a lot of options. You may be pleasantly surprised to find that a full-service carrier can actually get you from point A to B cheaper than a competing LCCs. Shop around!

CHAPTER II

Booking the Ticket

Booking a ticket for a flight is incredibly easy and incredibly complicated at the same time. There are many travel aggregator websites that allow you to not only book a flight ticket, but cabs and hotels too. Airline websites offer these add-ons as well, but the main benefit of aggregator sites is that you can compare prices between different airlines and choose the flight that is the cheapest, or the most convenient.

It is prudent to open up multiple tabs of these websites while buying a ticket; at the same time, keep the booking page of the airline open as well. Many a time, the airline site offers flights at cheaper rates: after all, the travel aggregator sites have to make their money *somewhere*.

There's also the good old-fashioned travel agent, but they are fast becoming an extinct species. Travel agents are fine if you don't have a computer at home or in the office, or if your office has an approved travel agent who gets the bills passed smoothly. Its your choice, really.

Cheapest? Or Best?

While comparing flights, be on the lookout for the number of stops and the total transit time. The cheapest ticket from one place to another may well take you via a third place which is totally off the track and adds hours to the travelling time. On the other hand, a direct flight many cost a couple hundred rupees more, but get you there direct. A few years ago, when travelling to London from Bangalore, I had an option of flying the cheap route that would take me 26 hours to reach, including a 14-hour layover at Doha. A direct flight which takes 10 hours was just about 4000 rupees dearer. I naturally chose the latter.

Sometimes, a hopping flight is inevitable. If it involves just a stop at an intermediate location, there's nothing to bother about except a slight loss of time. If on the other hand it involves a change of aircraft, or—in the worst case, a change of carriers—be prepared for a lot of walking and waiting at the luggage carousel. A change of carriers is best avoided if the gap between flights is less than two hours, since a delay in the earlier flight will not guarantee that you reach before the next flight departs. More importantly, the other carrier has no obligation to refund your ticket, so such a delay could prove very costly.

When to Book

Ticket pricing is quite complicated; prices rise in slabs, and as the number of bookings increases, prices rise. It's safe to say though that the earlier you book your ticket, the lower the prices are likely to be. If you are planning a holiday, booking tickets should generally be your first priority. I would say though that as long as you book a month or more in advance, you'll get a pretty good deal. If your leave slot falls in peak holiday season, try to book three months early instead.

Peak holiday season in India depends mainly upon school holidays – April to June, then again during Dussehra break and finally during the short Christmas/New Year break. Flights to Srinagar are usually oversubscribed during the summer months, while Port Blair visits require advance planning between January and May. Be aware of long weekends coming up, where people leave the city in droves, some of them by car, but many by air. Midweek flights are usually easier to book on than weekend flights.

Keep a weather eye out for special deals by airlines. These deals are usually one-offs and available for a discrete period (usually the off-season, say between July and October). There's also a very short window in which to buy the tickets, so you need to get to your PC *now* if you want to avail that special deal. Bookings usually start at midnight, so if you read about it in the morning paper, you may already be too late! One way of getting around this is to 'Like' the airlines' Facebook pages so that the notification comes to you as the advert is launched.

Personally, I'm not a fan of these one-off fares; they lure you into buying a ticket you had no intention of buying in the first place. You are almost guaranteed *not* to get them, as they're generally just one or two per flight; and if you do, it's because you lost a night's sleep blearily punching away at your laptop's keyboard. Then, you have to work your holiday plans around these dates, and if your boss refuses leave, then these non-refundable tickets are not worth the paper they're (not) printed on.

Finally, a middle-of-day flight is likely to be emptier than an early morning or late evening flight.

If being on time is important, you might like to do a little homework first to find out if your flight is likely to be late. Don't go completely by airline advertising as that can be misleading. The DGCA website and many other travel sites maintain statistics on flight delays, not just by airline but flight as well. Apps such as FlightAware and FlightRadar24 are useful tools to have on your smartphone. Of course, a simple search such as "flight delay statistics my-flight-here" may be as useful.

Dates are Important!

Having homed in on a travel date, take a look at your departure time. International flights usually leave after midnight, so it is very important to check the date *and* time of your flight. If a flight is leaving at, say, 12:30 AM, you need to reach the airport by 10:30 PM *the previous day*. Make full use of your mobile phone's calendar to have those alarms on tap.

There are various apps that allow you to store your ticket and boarding pass on the phone, and even set alerts for you. If you are a forgetful sort of person, make full use of them. You'd be surprised at how many people have missed their flight because they miscalculated their departure date and time!

Time Zones and the 24-hour Clock

If travelling abroad, its equally important to check the date and time *as per the local time zone*. The departure time is usually shown in the local time of the departure airport, while the arrival time is the local time at the destination.

To avoid confusion, tickets often show time in the 24-hour clock. This means that 1:00 PM is shown as 13:00, while 11:00 PM is shown as 23:00. Midnight comes up as 00:00, so a time of 00:35 means a flight that departs 35 minutes after midnight. To convert from the 12-hour clock to the 24-hour one, simply add twelve to whatever PM it is. Voila!

The 24-hour clock is often shown without the colon, so 1:00 PM could also be shown as '1300', '1300h' or '1300hrs'.

Documentation Is Vital

Passport, visa, proof-of-ID, ticket... make sure all your important documents are there with you. I carry my passport at all times in my carry-on bag. If travelling abroad, get your cash cards for the local currency and some hard cash as well. I find that my credit cards work beautifully and the nominal service charge actually makes them cheaper to use than pulling out cash from the local ATMs. Plastic is generally accepted anywhere in developed countries, but if going to developing nations, it would be a good idea to carry ready cash.

Is a Printout necessary?

While on the subject of tickets, there's no need really to print out domestic tickets any more – the CISF personnel at the entrance to all airports happily accept seeing the ticket on you phone, tablet, laptop... whatever it is that you're carrying with you. My 70-year old mother-in-law too pooh poohs the 'inane' idea of carrying paper tickets! Since 3G may not always work at the airport entry gate (phone connectivity is surprisingly poor around airports because of the vast open spaces) she prefers to take a screenshot of her eTicket that she can show to the security staff. My wife on the other hand takes a screenshot because she's never sure when her old phone's WiFi may give up on her.

In case of a problem though, you can always approach your airline's ticketing counter for a hard copy, but be prepared to shell out a hundred bucks or so for a printout.

While travelling abroad, I would definitely recommend a printout, though at most places, one can walk into an aircraft terminal unhindered.

Choosing your Seats (Yes, you can do that!)

Today's all-economy low cost aircraft have dispensed with First and Business classes in an effort to maximise volumes. What you get on board are seats that look absolutely alike. Yet, there are minor variations in some seats that make them more desirable, so you may like to consider pre-booking a seat to avail their benefits.

On the most common single-aisle domestic jet aircraft (the Airbus A320 and the Boeing 737) there are usually three rows of seats that offer a little extra. The first row in any aircraft has the illusion of extra leg space; the fact is that it usually has the same as any other row, but appears more spacious because there is no seat back staring you in the face. Knowledgeable passengers choose this row not so much for the leg space but because it's the first row, so they are usually the first to disembark. Mind you, this is not much of a perk if you have check-in baggage, or if you're disembarking by stairs and going to the terminal by bus. Some of the overhead baggage space is also usually occupied by emergency equipment, so you may just have to put your cabin baggage a couple of rows behind – another downer.

The emergency exit rows are preferred rows too – the seats have significantly greater legroom. The US Federal Aviation Authority for example mandates that the seat pitch (the distance between one row and the next) should be at least 36 inches, whereas the seat pitch in economy is usually 30 inches. However, these come with limitations; for example, if the emergency exit row is the leading of two such rows, the forward row seats do not recline, so if you choose that option, you will be forced to sit upright throughout the flight, or slump forward for a more relaxed posture. This isn't really as bad as it sounds, especially for short sectors, as airline seats have a reasonable built-in recline; in any case, most economy seat reclines are restricted to about 3 inches. So if you are a tall person and the rear emergency exit row seats are all taken, go for it!

There is however a caveat when booking these seats. You have to be of a certain minimum or maximum age, able bodied, able to lift 15 kgs or so (the weight of the emergency exit door) and—most importantly—be willing to operate the door in case of an emergency. This is an inviolable safety regulation, and since the airline has no knowledge at the time of booking whether you meet the above requirements or not, the cabin crew on board have complete authority over whether you can actually occupy those seats.

Since they offer extra legroom, they also cost extra, so be willing to fork out money for the added comfort. If you have paid the cost but do not meet the safety criteria, the airline is under no obligation to return you the money you paid, no matter how much you whine on social websites afterwards.

Then there are the two rows that are best avoided. The row immediately ahead of the emergency exit row has standard seat pitch, but *does not recline*. Likewise, the last row in an aircraft, which also usually suffers from the problem of people lining up to use the washroom pushing their butts into your face (if you happen to be in the aisle seat).

If you've booked a window seat to enjoy the view, you may be disappointed for a lot of reasons. First, the windows are very small and offer a very limited view of the outside world. Then, they usually slope upwards, so you get to see more of the sky than the ground. And finally, in India the visibility is generally so poor that you may not get to see much anyway. If you still prefer a window seat, remember to go to the washroom before the flight starts, as clambering over two people in flight can be quite cumbersome.

However a window seat can be its own reward as sometimes the stunning vistas are worth it. At night, the strings of pearls of city lights can be quite pretty, and if you are a geography buff, you can actually distinguish which highway it is running below you, or which is the city you're passing by. Not quite Google Earth, but close enough! For me, the sight of passing thunderstorms with their embedded lightning bolts can be an awesome spectacle.

Many people prefer the aisle seat as they think they can stretch their legs out into the aisle. There's usually a problem with that, since aisles are narrow, and there's always a person or a cart moving by forcing you to frequently tuck your legs back in. The one benefit of an aisle seat is that its easy to go to the washroom.

Pre-booking Meals

Budget airlines offer you the option of booking a meal along with your ticket. While onboard food is not really high cuisine, it makes sense to book, especially if you are travelling with young children or have a healthy appetite. Pre-booked meals are always served first, so if you haven't pre-ordered and are feeling peckish, be prepared to let your stomach growl a while longer.

Airlines like to limit the amount of extra food carried on board—usually for the purpose of fuel saving—but also because that extra food, if unsold, goes into the dustbin, and is essentially a loss for the company. This also means—depending on where you're sitting—that the food may well finish by the time the cart gets to you, or that you will have to take what's left, not what you want.

Food prices for onboard meals are actually quite reasonable. A full meal can be yours for Rupees 300/- ($5). You pay substantially higher at any half-decent restaurant or even at the airport cafes. You usually end up paying higher for food on board if you hadn't booked it in advance, so all in all, pre-booking a meal—especially if your flight is at mealtimes—makes eminent sense.

If you are travelling abroad, a meal or two—depending upon the length of your flight—are generally catered for in the cost of your ticket. While booking your ticket, you have an option of selecting the kind of meal you would like to have. Most international carriers carry the local cuisine while operating into or out of the country, so there's no need to worry. Many carriers even offer the option of Jain meals, diabetic meals and other such special options, so select these options at the time of booking, and board without a care!

Special Assistance

Is your young child travelling alone? Are you sending your aged parents by air? Did your brother break his leg rock climbing on holiday? Then they require special assistance and the airline will be happy to provide it for you. Visually/hearing impaired passengers, and passengers with mental disability are all welcome on board, with certain caveats, of course. Rules for their carriage vary from airline to airline, so be sure to check with the airlines reservations office.

For an unaccompanied child below a certain age, the airline charges extra – in return, they accept your child outside the terminal, accompany him/her through check-in, security, boarding and till their seat in the aircraft, then do the same at the other end till your child is safely with a designated adult.

For adults with special needs, or that adventurous brother, airlines will provide a wheelchair and an assistant from car-to-car. Wheelchairs come all the way till the aircraft door and it is up to the passenger to decide whether (s)he needs the wheelchair to go down the ramp or whether (s)he can hoof it.

Passengers with seeing-eye dogs are allowed to get them into the cabin – the only case where animals are allowed in. Of course, the dog has to be trained, vaccinated and muzzled, and the passenger needs to carry along a moisture-absorbent mat to put below the dog. For such visually impaired passengers, some airlines also offer safety instructions in braille.

Expecting ladies in the final stages of their pregnancy need a doctor's 'fit-to-fly' certificate since an aircraft interior is ...er ...not exactly a well-equipped labour room. In the unlikely event that your baby decides to come early though, be assured that cabin attendants are well-trained in the basics of delivery, and that there is usually (but not always) a doctor among the travelling passengers on board.

Many—but not all—airlines accept stretcher-borne passengers as well, but this requires the removal of a row of three or four seats and for the passenger to be accompanied with a medic and/or family member. All in all, this can work out to be quite expensive, but if you don't have a choice, you will need to tie up the requirements with the airline at the time of booking the ticket.

Travelling Abroad

If you're going abroad, there are a couple of additional factors you may like to consider. The first is, what aircraft to fly on. On domestic sectors or flights to neighbouring countries (UAE, Thailand, Singapore etc.), where flight times are less than 3 hours, the standard 30-inch seat pitch (the distance between two seats) will generally see you through without much discomfort. If however, you are tall, say 5'9" or more, and the flight is longish, you may want to select a plane with seat pitch of 32" or greater.

So why is the aircraft important? Because many airlines use their single-aisle aircraft otherwise employed on domestic sectors for international flights. Since larger aircraft like the Airbus A330, 340 and 380, or the Boeing 777 and 747 are longer-legged by nature, you can expect them to have a longer seat pitch. As a thumb rule, domestic LCCs go for a 30" seat pitch, while international economy seats on the wide-bodies average 32".

To be doubly sure, visit a website such as www.seatguru. com to get an idea of what seat pitch to expect on the aircraft/airline combination of your choice.

Of course, seat pitch alone is not the entire story; legroom is also dependent upon the thickness of the seat padding. A thicker seat back means less legroom for the same seat pitch, but that's hard to quantify. Then, there's seat width; single-aisle aircrafts have seat width that barely crosses 17", while wide-bodies go up the scale to 18.5" or so. If you think the one-and-a-half inches are inconsequential, visualise yourself sitting between two WWF wrestlers on a 10-hour transcontinental flight.

The second is about what you can carry and to where. Customs regulations vary from country to country and it pays to find out beforehand what you shouldn't take with you. Drugs for example are banned in more or less any country, but in certain countries their possession carries the death sentence. Codeine, commonly found in many OTC cough medications in the west is banned in the UAE. A simple Google search will bring up a website that tells you what a country will or will not accept at Customs.

Be especially careful while accepting packages from friends to carry abroad. Be prepared to interrogate them on the contents of the package even at the risk of offending them. It may be their stuff that's contraband, but you'll be the one cooling your heels in jail.

CHAPTER III

Packing Your Bag

There are two types of bags: carry-on and check-in. The names are self-explanatory: a 'carry-on' bag is what you 'carry on' board on your person, while a 'check-in' bag is what you 'check in' at the airport counter, then retrieve from the luggage carousel at your destination.

Weight = Cost

The amount of baggage you could carry without charge on a ticket has reduced considerably over the years. Today, an economy class passenger can carry a bag weighing up to 7 kgs on board, while check-in baggage is restricted to 15 kgs. For International flights this usually goes up to 20 or 30 kgs (economy class), depending upon the carrier, so if you likely to be carrying a lot of stuff, you may like to choose your carrier based on their generosity. Certain carriers offer weight incentives; students travelling abroad for example are generally allowed higher weight limits.

So why is weight such an issue with airlines? Well, quite simply, the heavier an aircraft, the more fuel it burns to carry that weight aloft. On a single-aisle medium-capacity aircraft such as the Boeing 737 or Airbus 320, the engines burn 30 kilograms extra fuel per hour of travel for every ton of extra weight hoisted aloft; on bigger aircraft such as the 777, its much more. Which means that on a Delhi-Bangalore flight, if every passenger packed 5 kilos extra, the aircraft would burn up an additional 80 kilos, or 5,000 rupees of fuel. That's the cost of one ticket on that flight. Multiply that by 1500 flights a day, 365 days a year and you get the picture. Forget the loss of profit to the airline; instead look at the environmental costs and ask yourself whether it is worth stuffing your bag with non-essentials.

This is why airlines are so particular about making you pay for the extra baggage. The cost per kilogram can be heavy, so don't pack a huge bag with the naïve assumption that a smile or threat will persuade the check-in counter to let you off. Instead, choose what you pack with care. You'd be surprised at how little you actually need.

Since you can carry up to 2 bags—one in the hold and one onboard—choose your luggage carefully. Synthetic fibre bags with retractable handles and at least one pair of wheels are pretty standard now. Many big manufacturers advertise bags with TSA-compatible locks – a useful feature if you travel frequently to the US, quite useless otherwise. Carry-on bags are usually restricted by size too, details of which are posted on every airline's website. You will also find metal frame bag sizers helpfully placed near airline check-in counters to allow you to determine whether your bag can be carried into the cabin. Some bag sizers have built-in weighing machines too. These bag sizers are also placed strategically at the boarding gate, and airline staff may ask you to confirm that your bag meets the requirements. If its oversized or overweight, off into the hold it goes, against all your protests. If your protests become, er... 'strong', the airline reserves the right to deny you boarding. Its much better to check your bags before you reach the check-in counter!

While packing, determine what you need, and what can be bought at the destination. Pack according to the weather. If you intend to carry a jacket, you can reduce weight by wearing it instead of packing it. Synthetic clothes are not only lighter, but also don't crumple easily. Your toilet kit should contain the smallest tube of everything from toothpaste to shaving cream and deodorant, not only to reduce weight but also because liquids in quantities greater than 100ml are not permitted on board for safety reasons. Consider reusing clothes instead of packing a pair for each day.

If on a holiday, nothing works better than a pair of jeans or cargoes that can be worn for 4-5 days. Take along throwaway cotton tees that can be discarded while returning. Ask yourself if you *really* need to carry that laptop or whether your smartphone or tablet will suffice for the duration.

There's one thing I carry at all times and that's basic medication. An analgesic, pain-reliever and anti-diarrhoea medication are a standard part of my medicine kit, apart from medication that I may be on from time to time. If staying at hotels, I also prefer to carry my own shampoo and soap, partly because of the tremendous waste of the complimentary hotel toiletries, but that's another subject altogether.

What Happens in Baggage Holding

Baggage handling at airport can be quite ...er... vigorous. While most modern airports rely on automated sorting systems, the bag's final journey from the belt to the pallet, or from the trolley to the hold still requires human intervention. Before you get all worked about about the baggage handlers tossing your luggage about, try keeping a 20-kg bag down ...gently. Then imagine stepping into the shoes of these guys who handle bags day-in and day-out for a living.

Its remarkably rare, but not unheard of, to see broken handles and cracked plastic bodies on those bags you paid a fortune for. If that worries you, then you should avail of those wrapping services that you find in most big airport, where your bag is wrapped in layers of cellophane before being deposited at the counter. I'd also recommend that if there's anything fragile you're carrying, you should either enclose it in layers of bubble wrap and surround it with soft clothing, or – better still – carry it in your handbag.

Dangerous Goods

The IATA manual that lays down regulations for carriage of dangerous goods is a 600-page tome. All airline websites display an abridged version of the regulations. Boards are also displayed at check-in counters. If you still have any doubt about whether an item you are carrying is dangerous or not, don't hesitate to call the airline for clarifications.

There are many, many items that may seem perfectly normal in daily life, but can be dangerous onboard an aircraft. Take Copra (dried coconut) for example; it's a staple of south Indian cooking, but the combination of the oil concentration and the heat it generates while drying in confined spaces can actually cause Copra to combust spontaneously! Carriage of Copra is strictly prohibited, and no amount of pleading will persuade the check-in staff to allow it onboard.

As I mentioned earlier, liquids in any quantity greater than 100ml is usually suspect. Clear liquid, which does not trigger any X-ray alarms could well be explosive. That's why security personnel do not allow you to carry water bottles through. If you don't want to pay inflated prices for water bottles at the airport, carry an empty bottle along and fill it up from the drinking spigots once through security (beware though, that tests have shown these spigots to carry large concentrations of bacteria). If you're carrying milk bottles for your child, security staff may well ask you to drink some to prove its not something dangerous masquerading as milk.

The one exception to this liquid rule is alcohol. Up to 5 litres of alcoholic beverages can be carried on board *in their retail packing*. However, since drinking is not permitted on board domestic flights, airlines may have more stringent rules about, say, allowing them only with their seals intact.

Aerosols are considered dangerous since they could explode at altitude due to the pressure differential. However, hair sprays or deodorants in small quantities do not pose a problem.

Certain items that could be dangerous in confined quarters due to air rage are also not permitted on board. Pepper spray, ammunition cartridges, camping stoves with fuel, nail files, scissors and knives are examples of these, and no amount of persuading the security staff that you need that knife to cut your baby's apples before feeding time will work. These are best put in your check-in baggage. Some of these, such as pepper spray cannot be carried in check-in baggage either because of their potential harmful effects if their cans get punctured.

What To Carry

Many airlines also make concessions on additional baggage that can be carried on board – laptop bags and ladies handbags are two such examples. Please don't abuse this privilege by stuffing these bags with extraneous items, then fighting with other passengers about overhead storage. You see, overhead bins have a weight limit too; after all, they're made of lightweight composites themselves. Don't believe me? Stand on tip-toes and read the decals pasted in these bins.

Identifying Your Baggage

There have been many instances of travellers who landed at their destination, went to the luggage carousel, found their bag and drove off home, only to realise later that its someone else's. They then wasted half a day and a hefty amount of money, heading back to the airport, returning that bag and collecting their own.

This problem is much more common than you might assume – after all, if 500 bags from two flights are coming off the luggage carousel, the chances that two of them are the same model and colour of the same manufacturer are quite high.

There are many simple tricks to ensure that doesn't happen. The simplest of course, is to read the barcode tag to confirm your name is on it. If it isn't your bag, put it right back on the carousel. But what's to be done about bags that you carry on board, that don't have these barcodes? I mark my bags with special tags and write my name on them with golden marking ink, while my wife usually ties a bright coloured bow to the bags' handles for instant recognition. There are many ways to make your bag unique – pick one that suits you.

CHAPTER IV

At The Airport

What's an Airport Like?

Just like railway stations vary in size and complexity from the small, single-platform rural station to the humongous 15-platform metros, so do the airports. They all have many basic things in common though.

Arrivals are segregated from departures, usually by having them on different levels. Commonly, departures are on the upper level, as this allows passengers to go through check-in, security and into the aircraft through the aerobridge all at the same level. Passengers disembarking from an aircraft through the aerobridge usually need to descend a level or two to get through immigration and customs and past the duty-free (if travelling international) before reaching the luggage carousel and the exit.

At large international airports, there are usually multiple terminals, segregated by various classifications. At Delhi for example, Terminal 1D handles domestic departures of low-cost carriers (Go Air, IndiGo and Spicejet), Terminal 1C handles their arrivals, while the new Terminal 3 handles domestic flights of full-service carriers and international flights of all carriers.

In Mumbai, the old terminal handles domestic operations of all carriers, including full-service carriers such as Air India, Jet Airways and Vistara, while the new Terminal 2 handles international operations only. There is a move by IndiGo to take over the old terminal for its exclusive use; this implies that all other carriers will have to shift to terminal 2. If this happens, this will be a first for India, but is quite common practice elsewhere in the world.

In Amritsar, Bangalore, Chennai, Goa and Kolkata, the terminal is common, but international arrivals and departures are often segregated horizontally. This can lead to some absurdly comical situations at times; an aircraft arriving at Bangalore from a foreign destination disembarks its passengers through the aerobridge, but once its customs clearance is done and it has to operate a domestic flight, the aerobridge is removed and passengers have to embark using stairs!

At smaller airports without aerobridges, the terminal may consist of a small single-storey building with the arrivals and departures segregated horizontally. There are usually no aerobridges and passengers walk or take a bus to the aircraft.

Airport layouts vary hugely. Simple airports such as Bangalore, Hyderabad and Chennai have one long terminal with aircraft parking nose-in for aerobridge access. High-density airports such as Bangkok, Delhi and Hong Kong use piers to squeeze in more aircraft within the same land area. This design entails lots of walking, so travelators (horizontal or inclined escalators, also known as moving walkways) are provided for passengers to reach their gates without too much inconvenience. Very large airports such as Dubai, Kuala Lumpur and London Heathrow have multiple concourses set out as islands; access to these concourses is through travelators or even trains that run below the apron.

Walking from the car park to the terminal building, a passenger enters the 'landside' of the airport. This is the area in the terminal that is open to all – passengers can buy a last-minute ticket here, catch a bite, and check in. Beyond the security gates is the 'secure holding area' where a passenger stays between security and boarding the aircraft. Since this is essentially forcible confinement, airports go at great lengths to make these areas comfortable for passengers. So you'll find plenty of ways to spend money here: restaurants, cafés, duty-free shops, bookstores, curio shops, lounges, children play areas, massage chairs and of course the obligatory toilets, smoking lounges, water fountains and seating. Singapore's Changi airport has gardens, swimming pools and even a waterfall!

Many airports have hotels within the airport complex so that passengers transiting through can book rooms and catch a much-needed rest on real beds. Delhi has the Aerocity which is a 5-minute metro ride from the terminal and contains a multitude of hotels; Bangalore airport is opening a hotel that is across the car park.

Reaching the Airport

Airlines do *not* run on Indian Stretchable Time. Their schedules are so tight that even a 5-minute delay can cascade into a one-hour delay by the last flight of the day. On-time performance is a critical yardstick of airline efficiency, so pushing a flight out on time takes centerstage. In fact, there's an airline in India that actually advertises its on-time performance as the reason to choose it!

As a result of this near-fanatical approach to time management, airlines require the passenger to reach the check-in counter at least 45 minutes before departure, and can be quite ruthless in denying boarding without chance for refund if a passenger reaches even a few seconds after the counter is closed.

I usually give myself an extra 15-minute buffer and try to reach the airport at least one hour before scheduled departure. If my route is prone to traffic jams, I add another buffer to the travelling time. I then set three alarms on my phone – the first, 45 minutes before I have to leave home as a reminder to get ready, the second at 5 minutes to departure which tells me its time to get into the lift, and the third at one hour to departure, to assess whether I'm close enough to the airport to make the counter on time, or whether I need to call the airline and rebook my flight.

All over the world, you can enter an airport and go right up to the check in counter without having a ticket with you. Indian airports are probably unique, in that entry into the airport premises needs proof that you are a genuine traveller. Luckily, the CISF (Central Industrial Security Force) staff now recognise e-tickets, so the email on which your ticket was sent, or its PDF copy, is enough for them to let you in.

Speeding Up Your Check In

IF you're rushed for time, there's another option called web check-in, but this comes with its own caveats. Some airlines permit web check-in only if you don't have check-in baggage; others expect you to check-in much earlier than counter closure. Web check-in has its own benefits, for example, you can reach the airport a mere 30 minutes before departure, skip the check-in line, then move directly to security and into the aircraft. Read up on an airline's web check-in requirements to maximise its benefit.

Some airlines offer express lines at an additional cost. These lines are much smaller than the regular check-in line and can save you valuable time. However, they have to be booked in advance and are therefore not of much use if you find yourself stuck in traffic on the way to the airport. I would strongly recommend use of these lines by senior citizens and those who are claustrophobic.

Many airports now offer kiosks where you can operate a touch screen to print your boarding card. These kiosks are useful if you don't have check-in baggage, else you might as well stand in line.

Reaching the check-in counter, hand over your ticket to the staff, then load your check-in baggage onto the luggage conveyor. There is usually a weighing machine on that part of the conveyor, and a readout of your bag's weight on the counter. While the check-in staff are printing out your boarding pass and baggage tags, pick up a tag for your carry-on bag and attach it. This is very important in India, as you will see later. After your check-in bags are tagged, a stub from the tag will be attached to the rear of your boarding pass. This will allow you to crosscheck at your destination that the bag you offloaded from the carousel is indeed yours.

Keep Your Boarding Pass Safe

A ticket allows you entry into the airport; a boarding pass authorises you to enter the aeroplane. Once a boarding pass has been issued, the ticket serves no use whatsoever. Even LTC claims require production of the boarding pass to prove that the flight was actually taken. Moreover, its stamped by security personnel as an indication that you have been scrutinised and are safe to board. So its important that you keep it safe.

I recommend folding it along the tear line and keeping it in the inner coat or jacket pocket or a shirt pocket. Avoid keeping it in the back pocket of your jeans, or putting any other items with it, since pulling out that other item can inadvertently pull this out too. Ladies, please designate a handy, accessible compartment in your handbags where these boarding passes can be stored; you'll need to pull them out often. Take them out of your handbag and put them in the seat pouch in front of you before you buckle up, as you may need to produce it to get your pre-booked meal.

My wife remembers watching a drama unfold: a hungry woman who wanted her meal, who then demanded – rather forcefully – that the helpful cabin attendant search in her bag's pockets for her boarding pass. This pocket. No? Okay, try that one. Well, maybe its in the *third* one. Guess what happened? The cabin attendant told her, quite politely, that she'll be back as soon as she's finished with the other passengers. That lady went hungry for quite a while.

The boarding card is also required at transit stops to prove to security that you are going on the next leg, or— while disembarking—to prove that this is actually your stop. Keep it handy as you alight; it's an all too common sight to see fifty passengers wait patiently while the passenger at the exit fishes around their bag and pockets looking for that elusive boarding card. These security measures were implemented in the past when passengers left an aircraft at an interim stop, leaving explosive-laden hand baggage on board.

Security

Having sent your luggage packing and gotten your boarding card, its now time to get into the departure area. To get to that, you have to go through a security check of you and your baggage. You'll find there are separate lines for ladies, gentlemen and airport staff. If you are travelling as a family, wives and daughters will have to go through the ladies' line, so whoever has the boarding passes should hand it to them beforehand.

At smaller airports, there may not be a separate line for airport staff; instead, there will be a sign telling you that Crews have priority. If, after a long shuffle, you reach the front of the line, and a crewmember politely says 'excuse me', please don't give him/her dirty looks or try and force your way ahead. Its quite likely that they are the pilots of your very flight, and by delaying their arrival at the aircraft, you are in fact delaying yourself, or—worse—causing them to hurry and miss out on an important safety check. Do the polite thing for your own sake, and allow them to pass.

Before reaching the front of the line, you have to empty your pockets of anything metallic, which means your phone, wallet and keys. Put them in your carry-on bag's pouch or if you don't have a carry-on bag, pick up a tray and put them in there. At many international airports, security staff also insist that you remove your belt, shoes and jewellery – anything that could have a trace of metal in it. If the Door Frame Metal Detector (DFMD) still beeps as you pass through, you will be subjected to a very thorough screening by a handheld metal detector, or even by a backscatter machine if the airport has it.

Laptops, other electronic items (cameras, video recorders, game players etc) and jackets also have to be put in the tray. Remember to first remove your boarding pass from the jacket pocket if that's where you had stored it. These trays and your carry-on bag are to be put in the X-ray machine tray before you proceed for your own check.

In India, there is no particular need to be thorough about removing all metallic items from your body before passing through the DFMD, since you will be subjected to a check by handheld scanners anyway. Still, its advisable to put all metallic stuff in your bag before you walk through the DFMD. Stand with your arms and legs akimbo so that the security personnel can do their job quickly and efficiently. The wand is not supposed to touch you; rather it is supposed to be moved about 2 inches away from your body. If the security staff rubs their wand all over, you are well within your rights to complain to the supervisor.

For a hassle-free security check, you may like to read the 'Travel Tips' section on the Bureau of Civil Aviation Security's website (www. bcasindia.nic.in).

The Great Indian Tag Stamp

Screening done, it is now time to collect your items from the X-ray machine. This is where the baggage tag comes into play. Around the world, a baggage tag is meant for you to write your name and contact number, so that if you leave it on board inadvertently, it can be quickly returned to you. In India however, it is meant for security staff to stamp it as an indication that the bag has passed through X-ray. So, as you pick up your bags from the X-ray machine, make sure that they've been stamped with the current date. If you miss out on that step, you'll have to go back to security from the boarding gate, just to have the bag stamped!

The Endless Wait – Delays and How to Handle Them

Delays Happen. For a hundred different reasons. The weather could be bad, and not necessarily where you are. Congestion in the air, or on the ground. VIP movement. Runway closure due to an accident. Aircraft unserviceability. On-Time Performance, which can touch 95% or more during good months, can fall to 70% or less during the winter fog season, or during monsoons. This means that one of every five domestic flights you take during the winter is likely be delayed.

So, rather than chafe at delays, it is much better to anticipate them and be prepared. Occasionally, a delay is passed on by SMS up to a day or two earlier, which allows you to reschedule your departure plans accordingly. These delays are generally due to route restructuring or coping with a temporary shortage of aircraft, as may happen when one goes down unexpectedly for technical reasons.

Much more frequently though, delays occur after you have already set out, or once you reach the airport. Since there is nothing you can do about it, you may as well make the most of it.

Get your earphones and make sure your smartphone is loaded with your favourite music. Get a book along, or two, or ten. I carry my iPad and that has all digital editions of all my magazines and a few books to boot – no bulky paper for me. I see many people who sit down and finish off some office work on the computers. And if you're fed up with electronics, grab a coffee, something to eat, or find a comfortable chair to crash out on.

If you plan to catch a nap, try and do it at one of the chairs at your departure gate. That way, if you're still sleeping when boarding nears completion, its easy for gate staff to spot you and assume that you are the 'missing' passenger they are looking for. Its also prudent to set an alarm for 20 minutes before scheduled departure time.

Finally! The Boarding

The time between which the aircraft reaches the aerobridge or gate and opens its doors for disembarking passengers, to the time that the doors are shut for pushback is called the *turnaround time*. One of the ways in which airlines make their meagre profits is to squeeze in as many flights a day the aircraft can fly; and since flight times cannot be played around with, the turnaround times get compressed. Airlines usually work on a turnaround time of 25-30 minutes, and in some cases, even 20 minutes.

In these 20-30 minutes, a hundred and eighty passengers have to disembark, the cabin and toilets have to be cleaned, fresh food and water have to be taken on board, the outgoing cargo has to be offloaded, incoming cargo has to be stowed, fuelling has to be done, and finally, a hundred and eighty passengers have to embark, stow their luggage and take their seats. This last process is often the slowest.

In keeping with the silent airport concept, boarding isn't usually announced nowadays. Instead, the flight status is displayed on big screens all over the terminal. The status usually goes from blank, to CHECK IN, SECURITY, BOARDING and FINAL CALL. When BOARDING lights up next to your flight, if you are not already at the boarding gate, you should be heading there. If the status changes to FINAL CALL, you better rush!

As boarding commences, gate personnel will often request you very politely to board as per your sequence. This is to ensure that boarding is done in the fastest possible manner. If boarding is through the aerobridge, passengers seated in the last rows are often asked to board first. If your seat is in the front rows, you can bide your time peacefully in your chair and read a few extra pages of that gripping novel you have in your hand. If however you're boarding a bus to head to an aircraft on a remote bay, you can stand in line at the time of your choosing.

Checking in and going through security is no guarantee that you will actually board your flight. Once the boarding line empties, staff members at the gate tally the number of checked-in passengers with the number who have boarded. If you aren't on the list of boarded passengers, the staff try to contact you on your cellphone. This doesn't always work – it seems that an unusually large number of passengers put their phones on silent while in the terminal! The staff will then page you – very reluctantly since this goes against the 'silent airport' philosophy – which too is usually not heard since the airport is anything but silent, and announcements are generally all too muddy.

Now, the other passengers have boarded, the staff have called you on your cellphone, then paged you, but you are still nowhere to be found. Will the flight wait for you? Absolutely not! Delaying a flight not only means a delay to the 100+ passengers already on board, but could lead to a cascading effect of delaying hundreds of passengers on the aircraft's subsequent flights over the rest of the day. What the staff will do instead is strike your name from the list, inform the Captain of the last-minute change to the load and trim and—if you have checked in baggage—they will identify your bag and get it offloaded. As you see your flight taxying out with you not on it, no amount of ranting at the staff will change anything. And, you won't even get a refund on your ticket.

So, its best to ensure that you're at the gate when boarding starts.

Airport Etiquette

At any given time, an airport could be milling with thousands of passengers and thousands more of airport and airline staff. Certain levels of behaviour are necessary to make everyone's journey pleasant.

The most common example of thoughtless behaviour witnessed at the airport is of passengers who plonk themselves right in the middle of a traffic stream. Hundreds of passengers weave past them on the way to various gates while they look for something in their handbag, talk over a cup of coffee, or fiddle with their zips. Obstructing traffic flow may just get you bumped and banged as people collide into you or trip over your luggage in their hurry to catch their flight. Get to the side to do your dawdling. That's common sense, right?

Then, there are those who go to the food court, pack a meal to go, find an empty seat at the gate to sit on, and after they're done with their meals, leave the chicken crumbs and paper cups dripping coffee dregs onto the seat. Look around you, people: there's a garbage can not more than 15 metres from where you are! Better still, find a table at the food court itself.

Its an established fact that the number of seats at a gate are usually less than the number of passengers waiting to catch the flight. All too often, they're taken up by handbags. Don't be fussy, keep your handbags on the floor – its generally clean enough to eat off – and leave the chair for some other passenger to sit on.

Most important, please stand in queue. Whether to enter the airport, check your baggage in, go through security, or to board the flight, queue, queue, queue. This is not a race!

CHAPTER V

On Board The Aircraft

Smile!

As you enter the aircraft, there's a well groomed cabin attendant waiting to greet you with folded hands or a cheery hello. They do that 800 times a day and it wouldn't kill you to smile back and say thank you. It lightens the mood and sets the tone for the rest of the flight.

Don't waste any time chatting them up though. The flight is on a tight schedule and they'd rather you stow your bag in the overhead locker and take your seat as soon as possible. Aisles in the aircraft are barely broad enough for you, so the longer you take settling down, the longer it will take the people behind you to go past and take their own seats.

For this reason, many airlines insist on passengers sitting in the rear of the aircraft to board first – that way, a delay at the back does not affect other passengers coming in later. You'll often find gate announcements to this effect advising passengers from row numbers X to Y to come forward for the boarding. Many people still try to board first in the hope of grabbing the best overhead storage, but the airlines have gotten smarter and check your boarding pass before it gets scanned, so if you try to sneak in before your time, be prepared for a polite-but-firm shunt out of line.

Your CarryOn Bag Isn't Safe

So you've been through these many layers of security, and you're on board an aircraft with a captive set of fellow passengers, with your handbag right above your head. It couldn't get any safer than this, right? Wrong! Baggage gets shifted around by those who come in later and try to adjust their bags in the overhead bin. A partly open zip with the edge of a smartphone sneaking out may be just too tempting for another passenger to lay their hands on. It's better to keep it in your pocket instead. Try and keep your laptop or any other precious cargo behind a locked zipper; better still, take it out of the bag and keep it in the pocket in front of you.

Sit Where You're Told To

As it turns out, the seat is cramped and you're crushed between two hulks with no place to rest your elbows. You spy an empty seat that looks way more comfortable and call the cabin attendant to ask if you can sit there. You're surprised, and a little hurt, when she refuses.

The reasons for the refusal are many. For starters, boarding may not have finished yet, and its possible to have a passenger come up later and raise Cain because you're in their seat. Also, at this time, the crew are busy getting the passengers seated and their luggage stowed, so they really have no time to go forward, get the load manifest and see if that particular seat is indeed empty. Or, it could be a 'premium' seat and the cabin attendant gives you a nasty shock by demanding you pay up a fat wad to sit there (the first row, emergency exit rows, and sometimes even window seats fall into that category). And finally, believe it or not, but the place you sit determines the fuel efficiency of the aircraft!

Fresh Air Doesn't Come From the Window

In December 2014, a Chinese first-time traveller sitting in the emergency exit row decided it was too hot, and he should open the window to get some air. As he opened the emergency exit, the plane had to abandon the takeoff, causing another plane to be told to go around. The runway was blocked temporarily, the flight of course delayed, other flights at the airport severely affected as well and the passenger was hauled off by the police for endangering the flight. All this because he didn't know what the emergency exit was really for!

The cabin is essentially a giant metal tube that gets pressurised as the plane climbs. Windows on the plane *do not open* – they simply have a shade that slides down. On the ground on hot days the air conditioning may not work so well, so if you're feeling hot, look up, identify the blower that belongs to your seat and rotate and adjust it so that a steady stream of cool air falls on you. Soon after takeoff as the flow of air over the air conditioning packs kicks in, you'll be pampered by a lovely stream of cool air and may even have to turn the nozzle down a bit. Till then, patience.

Take an Electronic Break

Your first order of business after settling down in your seat should be to put your seatbelt on. My second order of business is usually to shift my phone and tablet onto flight mode. This is still a regulatory requirement on all airlines across the world and yes, if the aircraft you're in is old enough, your cellphone transmissions could jeopardise safety. In any case, soon after the aircraft is airborne, you'll be well outside cellular range and your phone will simply burn up energy trying to lock on to a signal.

There's another good reason why you should keep your cellphones and other electronic devices off and that's so that you can listen to the safety briefing.

Germophobes Beware

Everything in the aircraft is common-use – the seat, buckles, tray tables all have been handled or sat on by hundreds of passengers before you. If you are a germophobe, or particularly susceptible to infection, it would do you good to carry some antiseptic wet wipes with which to wipe down these items. Surprisingly, the light switch and overhead air vents carry a lot of germs with them, while the lavatory flush button actually trails close behind.

Safety is For Everyone

There are usually quite a few announcements once the passengers are seated. The first is a welcome PA that gives brief information on the impending flight, such as the crew introductions, the flight time, the cruise level the aircraft expects to fly at and expected weather enroute. The next—and most critical—PA in the course of the flight is the safety briefing. Finally, there's a sales pitch to buy products from the sky shop; this one is usually heard on LCCs.

Now, if you're a regular flyer, the safety briefing may seem like yet more mindless drivel to endure and the temptation to continue chatting with your neighbour or to tune out with some FM radio on your phone may be very strong. But, take a step back and consider this: if you succumb to the first temptation, there may be a first-timer travelling next to you who's unable to follow the briefing because of your continued conversation and may well be the one to block your way during an evacuation because he can't understand what's going on. In the second case, your memory may play tricks on you and you could find yourself heading in the wrong direction during an emergency evacuation simply because you forgot you were on another aircraft than the one you had flown in previously!

If this too sounds like drivel, take a step back and put yourself in an imaginary evacuation. Picture this: there's thick smoke in the cabin, you are choking on it, your exit into the aisle is blocked by the unconscious 140-kg passenger in the aisle seat, there are people clambering over you to get out, in the aisle there's another traveller who's trying to drag his hand baggage along, the heat from the fire creeping towards you is starting to sear your skin and suddenly you don't know where the nearest exit is because you are completely disoriented. In a minute or so, the smoke will completely overwhelm you and you will asphyxiate to a horrible, choking death.

Time to unplug and take the briefing seriously.

CHAPTER VI

Taxying Out

Now that you've stowed your bag in the overhead locker, settled down in your seat, put your phone to airplane mode and started listening to the briefing more attentively, you'll notice that the aircraft has started pushing back from its bay with a gentle nudge. Or else, the engines are being started in the bay itself, if the aircraft will be taxying out under its own power. You might notice that the air conditioning goes off briefly, as all the air is diverted for starting the engines (yes, most engines employ air starters), so if you're feeling hot, you can open the overhead ventilation nozzles some more. Thankfully, this interlude is brief and the air conditioning comes back on line as soon as the engines are started.

To save fuel and time, the pilots may elect to start just one engine, while the other one is started during taxi. The cabin is actually so well shielded from engine noise that you may not even notice it.

As the briefing finishes, the cabin crew prepare the cabin for takeoff. This means that they wrap up their safety briefing, then go around checking that seat belts are fastened, seats are upright, window shades are up and tray tables are closed. If you get irritated by their insistence on your doing any of these, remember that all of these are necessary for your own safety. Should an incident occur on takeoff, your seatbelt might save you from the risk of a serious injury. Should you need to evacuate, the inclined seat and lowered tray table will hinder your exit just when time is critical. And if your window shade is down, you may be unwittingly stepping out into a conflagration because the people inside were unable to look out and confirm that side was safe to exit on. Ignoring these simple safety instructions could literally be the difference between life and death.

This is the wrong time to buzz the bell and ask the cabin crew for a glass of water, a pillow, a newspaper or some such frivolous request. The cabin attendant has other safety issues to worry about and is likely to ignore you. If she doesn't, that momentary distraction could cause a significant delay in the departure, since the pilots will not initiate takeoff till they have confirmation that everyone—including the cabin crew—is seated. Every two-minute delay results in another 20 kgs of fuel burn, and that is likely to reflect in your next higher ticket price! Keep those requests to yourself until the seat belt sign is switched off a few minutes later. Of course, if it is a safety-related issue, then by all means buzz the crew.

The Wings are *meant* to flex

As the aircraft taxies out, you look out the wing and see that they are doing a mighty jiggle. That's because the wings have a large amount of flexure built in, and the jiggle is the inevitable result of taxying over the expansion joints.

The aircraft is actually out of its element on the ground, as the landing gear does not provide the same kind of stability that a car's wheels do, nor do the shock absorbers in the landing struts work that way. Their primary job is to absorb the impact of the landing without passing too much of it to the airframe. Turns are restricted to a mere 20 kmph, while speeds on the wide-open taxi tracks top out at 50 kmph or so. As for comfort, that's the runway's job. Once the aircraft is airborne, the landing gear has no role to play till landing, so its tucked away into the aircraft belly.

Take off

You've probably heard that most accidents occur during takeoff and landing. That's true, but before you start hyperventilating at the thought, remember that an accident by itself is a very rare occurrence. What you should be prepared for, is how to get out in case an evacuation occurs. That's when paying attention to the safety brief will come in handy.

So why is a takeoff the riskiest part of the flight? For a number of reasons. With both engines running at full thrust, if one engine fails, the thrust asymmetry causes the aircraft to yaw, and it could go off the runway. At high speed (but before the critical takeoff decision point), an engine failure results in a high-speed reject which throws you forward in your seats, hence the seat belts. Imagine you're sitting in your car and need to slam on the brakes. Now imagine you're not wearing a seatbelt. A high-speed reject is somewhat like that.

At the critical decision point, if an engine fails, the pilot has to make a split-second decision on whether to continue the takeoff or to abort. If the decision to abort is made a fraction of a second too late, the aircraft risks going off the end of the runway; if the decision is made to continue, the aircraft is now trying to get airborne with half the usual power available and the margins to obstacles on the ground (trees, poles, hillocks...) are considerably reduced. Then, the pilot has to nurse the aircraft around and get it to land.

If its raining, these safety margins are reduced; if its snowing, the margins reduce even further. If there's a thunderstorm in the vicinity, the chances of windshear reducing these margins further become quite strong. So yes, a takeoff is critical.

Did I tell you not to hyperventilate? I still am. *All* the above scenarios are practiced by the pilot and co-pilot once every six months in a simulator. The two sweat-wringing sessions are not considered complete till the pilots have demonstrated their abilities to handle them and fly the aircraft back to a safe landing. All these exercises are simulated considering the most critical and demanding conditions.

Modern engine are solidly engineered and can run for hundreds of thousands of hours between failures. Windshear encounters are rare occurrences too, not least because pilots have access to predictive windshear sensors and elect to delay takeoffs if a likely windshear exists. So, in effect, they practice and practice for events that they may never see in their entire flight careers.

Go ahead, feel safe. But prepare yourself mentally for evacuation.

Evacuate! Evacuate!

This is the call you'll usually hear in case an evacuation is required. It may be modified conditionally, so for example if you hear 'Evacuate Left' it probably means there's a fire or smoke on the right side and its unsafe to get out of the exits on that side of the aircraft.

You'll probably get adequate advance notice of evacuation, especially before a landing but it may be considerably shorter in case a takeoff is aborted. Even after the aircraft comes to a complete halt, it could be a while before your hear the 'Evacuate' command over the PA system. That's because the pilots up front are making the aircraft safe for evacuation (like shutting down engines and discharging the fire extinguishers for example). Its also much more likely that an evacuation will not happen at all, so please remain seated till such time the evacuation call is sounded.

There are some golden rules to follow during an evacuation, most of which are told during the safety briefing, but which we tend to gloss over in favour of our newspapers, books and music. In the interest of saving your life, its worthwhile though to commit them to memory.

For starters, most evacuations are precautionary, so its important to remember not to *panic.* Panic has been found to be the number one killer in evacuations.

Even if the emergency is real, keep in mind that globally, *every* aircraft is certified for evacuation by a full load of passengers within 90 seconds with only half the exits available. 90 seconds may seem like a very long time when you are actually inside the aircraft waiting to get out, but its actually enough to get you out before the situation starts spiralling out of control.

Now, I cannot emphasise this enough: It's very, *very* important to leave your belongings behind. A suitcase can block your exit; a laptop bag can become a hurtling projectile on the steep escape slide. Your toothbrush and underwear are replaceable and certainly not worth risking your life over. Get yourself out of your seat and to the nearest exit as soon as possible, leaving your belongings behind. In all probability, you'll be united with it soon. And *please* don't be tempted to go back for your stuff because someone else is lugging theirs along.

If you see smoke start to build up, get down on your belly, since the hot smoke rises to the top of the cabin first, then makes its way down as it gets thicker. Use the fluorescent strips to guide you to the nearest exit.

As you reach the slide, don't hesitate, just jump. They may seem steep and scary, but are designed for you to land on your feet. If you are injured getting off the slide, its probably because you did something stupid like carrying your 'precious' bag or laptop along with you.

An evacuation by itself is an extremely rare occurrence, but when it happens, you should be prepared.

CHAPTER VII

The Flight

As the aircraft accelerates for takeoff, you're pushed back into your seat, and you get the impression that the aircraft is climbing uphill. This is completely normal and the uphill illusion is because you can't see ahead. The engine sound builds up to a crescendo and a lot of other parts jiggle and vibrate. This is normal too.

At some point, the aircraft 'rotates', meaning that it raises its nose to get off the ground. As the wheels leave the tarmac, you'll feel much of the vibrations, those induced by a less-than-mirror-smooth runway, disappear. You'll now feel another vibration – that of the wheels that are still spinning due to inertia. This too is completely normal. While the main wheels are braked automatically as they lift off the ground, the nose wheels don't, so they'll continue to rumble until the landing gear is raised into its bays. The landing gear itself makes quite a few noises when it is moving up into its bays. What's left now is the residual rumble from the extended flaps. In a minute or so after takeoff, as the flaps are retracted, the flight smoothens out and all that is felt is the throb of the engines at climb power.

The First 20 Minutes

Seat belt signs usually go off 3-4 minutes after takeoff. When they do, most people jump at unclipping them. Bad idea. Just as a road accident happens without prior warning, there are many times that an aircraft could fly into clear air turbulence without knowing of its existence. While rare, injuries due to turbulence do happen, and statistics have shown that most passengers who were injured were not wearing seat belts. So, keep those seat belts on, just as you would do in your car. The sign being switched off merely indicates that if you'd like to get some stuff down from your carry-on bag, or want to make a trip to the washroom, now is the time to do so.

This is also about the time that it is considered safe to get back to your electronic devices. In modern planes, 'no smoking' signs have been replaced with signs that say 'turn off electronic devices', not least because smoking is banned on board flights across the globe. You can put your electronic devices on, but you still need to keep your phone in airplane mode as its emissions could interfere with aircraft signals.

If there's weather in the climb, its quite possible that the seatbelt signs will stay on longer than the first few minutes. In case you're wondering why the cabin attendants can roam about while you can't, its because the airline is concerned about your wellbeing and would like to ensure that you get your food and drink. There's an acceptable level of risk that allows that cabin attendants to be mobile. Be assured though, that if the weather is likely to get really rough the cabin attendants will stop the service and strap themselves in. In fact, if you see that happening, or hear an announcement which goes something like "cabin crew to your seats, seat belts required", it might be a good idea to tighten your belt a couple of notches and finish that coffee fast.

How Food Service Works

Service starts within a few minutes of the signs being switched off. Once the service begins, the narrow aisle is blocked by the service cart as the cabin attendants move down the rows offering food and beverages. So if you need to go to the washroom to do your thing, the time is now. Keep in mind that the forward washroom is usually blocked for access to the cockpit, so you might have to go all the way to the rear. Please, please refrain from asking them to move the cart back all the way to the galley; you will be disrupting service to many, many passengers. Remember, it could be you who goes hungry on the next short sector.

Now for the service. If you had pre-booked your meal, in all likelihood you will be served first; if however you are on a full-service carrier, your meal will come to you row-wise. If you are flying international, you could be offered a choice of alcoholic beverages. When you accept them happily, keep in mind that the higher altitude gets you drunk faster, and any unruly behaviour could you land you in jail on arrival in a foreign country. Many airlines restrict the number of drinks to two anyway, unless you're in business class.

The food itself is not cooked on board. It comes on board pre-cooked, prepackaged and x-rayed. Most airlines have ovens on board to warm it up before serving it, while others elect to save weight by removing the ovens so what you get is cold foods (sandwiches and wraps) or something that can be cooked in boiling water, such as noodles. We once had a passenger who wanted his rotis hot off the stove one-at-a-time. No sir, not possible!

In the rarified atmosphere of the aircraft cabin, sealed yoghurt cups are ticking time bombs. Open them in the conventional fashion, and the contents are likely to burst forth in a fine pink spray (if its strawberry, yellow if mango) all over your pristine white shirt front. That's because the pressure inside the cup is at sea level, while the cabin pressure is the equivalent of flying at 8,000 feet. It's better to puncture the seal with your fork first – that equalises the pressure before you open it.

You get an entire meal on your tray. If you eat it, well and good; if you don't, it gets tossed out with the trash at the end of the flight. The one thing you can be assured of is that the food on your plate is quite fresh! And in case you were wondering, the reason most airlines prefer plastic cutlery is to save weight. Personally, I'm ambivalent about this argument, since the plastic comes from the same source that we are otherwise burning up in our engines, and after its long development process it gets thrown out after a single use.

Eating food off the plastic trays within the confines of your economy class seat without spilling anything on yourself can be quite entertaining. Enjoy the meal!

Turbulence

Turbulence is the one thing that you're almost guaranteed to encounter on any flight. Turbulence could range from a light chop to strong bouncing motions that could cause loose objects to fly around the cabin, though the latter occurrence is very very rare.

Close to the ground, thermals that result from uneven heating will cause your plane to bump and heave during takeoff and landing. These are usually strongest in the summer months. Passing thundershowers can cause microbursts and windshear that cause their own upheavals.

Passing through clouds on their way to the top, aircraft often encounter more turbulence. These clouds, that don't have sufficient moisture yet, don't show up on radar, so its almost impossible to avoid them at night. During the day, fields of clouds along the path make it difficult to manoeuvre without catching at least a bit of the turbulence generated by them.

Coming up to the usual cruising levels of 33,000 feet and above, the clouds usually thin out. Weather occurs only in the troposphere, so in the northern latitudes where the troposphere tops out at 29,000—33,000 feet, aircraft usually manage to fly above it. But then, the further south one goes, the higher the troposphere rises, topping out at about 60,000 feet over the equator. While flying over the Indian subcontinent in the pre-monsoon season (April to June), it is not unusual to see towering cumulonimbus clouds that go all the way up to this level.

Pilots use weather radar to avoid these massive clouds at all costs, since they pose extreme hazards by way of severe turbulence, hail and lightning. But while it is easy to dodge these massive-but-relatively-isolated clouds, other layers at these levels will still create mild turbulence.

Come the monsoon and levels of turbulence actually drop, as clouds change from the puffy cauliflower types to the more layered variety. However, some amount of mild turbulence is still to be expected.

Come winter, and a different kind of turbulence hits the skies over the Indian subcontinent. Its called Clear Air Turbulence, or CAT, and it happens when a fast-moving core of winds in the jet stream drags along slower wind on the outside, creating eddies which result in turbulence. CAT occurs between around 23,000 and 39,000 feet, the exact altitudes at which modern jet aircraft fly. The problem with CAT is that its impossible to see with the naked eye and pilots have to often rely on other indications and educated guesswork to predict it's presence.

Its widely accepted by scientists the world over that air turbulence is on the rise as a result of global warming. So while you brace yourself for more bumpiness, there's nothing to worry about as long as you keep that seatbelt on all the time.

Acceptable Behaviour On board

Now we come to the ticklish part. And that's how we conduct ourselves on board. Picture this: you've woken up at an ungodly hour, gone through check-in, perhaps immigration, then the tedious security check and the endless wait at the gate, and now you are shoehorned into a seat half the comfortable size, eating a tasteless airline meal within breathing distance of complete strangers. You're probably stressed out and edgy, right?

Now throw in unruly passengers, crying babies, queues at overflowing toilets and the flight can quickly become a nightmare. But here's the thing: if you want your neighbours to be considerate, it follows that you too should behave in an acceptable fashion. So, here's what I've learnt about acceptable behaviour from frequent flights as a passenger.

On the Seat. This is where you're going to be for a majority of the time of your flight, as will be the passengers to your left, right, ahead and behind. For starters, avoid using the front seat's headrest for support while getting in or out of your own seat – its like a whiplash for the passenger seated there. If that's really the only grip, hold and *ease* your weight on to it gently, and once in position, release it gently as well.

Hitting the front seat is not good! So now you're seated and find that your knees have difficulty adjusting. Well, jamming them into the seat back in front of you isn't the answer. Airline seats are thin, and by doing so, you're basically jabbing the guy seated in front of you in the back. Do that a few times and an altercation is almost guaranteed. If you splay your knees, you'll not only find that more comfortable, but you'll be able to adjust your knees next to the armrest.

Today's airline seats have restricted their recline to a mere 3 inches, yet even that is sometimes too much because of the small seat pitch. Laptop screens especially are in danger of snapping as they get crushed between the food tray and the seat back. If you feel like getting a shuteye, its always good form to inform the passenger behind you that you'll be reclining your seat. Then do it gently. Reclining the seat is prohibited during takeoff and landing, and also when the food service is underway.

Its always good to nod and say hello to your neighbours while getting in and its not a bad idea to engage them in polite conversation, but its much better to figure out when they're listening just because they are polite but not really interested. Then, its time to clam up.

Shaking your leg to an invisible beat whilst seated is a no-no. The rhythmic vibration transmits to the other seats as well. Don't play bongos or drums on the seat back in front of you either.

Taking off your shoes isn't a good idea. It's a known fact that people are so inured to their own body odours that they won't realise they've left some loose. Not so your neighbour, who's hit with the full impact of those armies of bacteria merrily producing cheesy gas.

There are a few things you can do to reduce the smell from your feet. Start by spraying them with deodorant or antiperspirant. Avoid synthetic socks. Wear leather or canvas shoes. Better still, wear open-toed sandals. Problem solved!

Speak Softly. Flying back from London to Bangalore, dinner had been served while we were over Europe and somewhere over the Caspian Sea it was time to catch up on some sleep to be fresh for a 6 AM arrival. So everyone settled down into their seats and even the cabin attendants withdrew discreetly into their galley area. Not so an old lady who was very chirpy as she carried out a 3-hour loud conversation with some long-forgotten friend. By the time we alit at Bangalore, I could have sworn there were at least 50 passengers who would have liked to gladly kill her but desisted out of good manners.

Its not just at night; odd departure times and hectic work schedules mean that many passengers take the opportunity to catch up on lost sleep in the course of a flight. Its only right that as fellow passengers we respect their needs and keep our conversations to unobtrusive volume levels – *Sotto Voce*, I believe is what the Italians call it.

Which brings me to the next issue. If you're watching a video on your laptop or listening to music on your phone, please, please, plug in the headphones first. Your neighbours may not share your enthusiasm for Salman Khan's Selfie Song or the latest Comedy Central clip.

You've bought a ticket, not the crew. In the past, pilots have been called 'glorified truck drivers'. Cabin attendants have been called worse. This kind of casteist attitude exists among a large section of the travelling public today, and carries with it a fair degree of unpleasantness on board. Cabin attendants are more often at the receiving end of this attitude. It's unfortunate how we treat those who look after our welfare.

Some kinds of behaviour is completely unacceptable. Sexual innuendo and harassment tops the list of crass behaviour. Snapping your fingers to call them is a complete no-no. If they ignore you, they have a complete right to. Calling them 'you' just doesn't cut it. You could politely say 'excuse me'; better still, try and call them by name – they all wear name tallies. And while they'll help you adjust you bag in the overhead locker, putting it there is not their job. If you leave your bag lying around in the aisle, security may well haul it off the aircraft before the doors close.

Before you decide to behave crassly, keep in mind that any kind of threatening and aggressive behaviour could result in a diversion to the nearest airport, with airport security waiting to haul you off the other end. At that moment, it doesn't matter who started it; by international law, you have become a threat to the aircraft's and its passengers' security. Instead, keep your peace and register a complaint with the airline on arrival.

Above all, the prime reason for the cabin crew to be on board is for your safety; serving meals and looking after your wellbeing is their secondary job.

Cleaning the toilet. The toilets on board, or 'washrooms' as we call them, are probably the cleanest toilets you'll ever see. Or at least they are, at the beginning of a flight. But do you know that they are the biggest source of infection on board? Not least because many who walk in to use them walk out leaving a mess behind.

I have seen urine sprayed all over the washroom floor. Washbowls that were filled with soapy water. Used diapers that some mother simply didn't bother to dump into the bins provided. Worst of all, I've seen and smelt (ugh!) someone else's faeces because that person couldn't be bothered to press a simple button.

There are no cleaners on board an aircraft; they come in only during the turnarounds, so there's no excuse for leaving the washroom dirty. As passengers, there are a few rules that everyone bar none should follow in the interest of cleanliness and germ contamination. Most of these rules are displayed pictorially in the washrooms themselves but bear repeating.

First, please latch the door after you enter. There's nothing more embarrassing and disgusting then to walk in on someone doing their thing. The latch is multipurpose; not only does it bar the entry of random strangers, it also flips on a little red note on the outside that says "OCCUPIED", letting others know they shouldn't be trying to barge in. It also changes a toilet sign on the front bulkhead from green to red, letting those in their seats know they need to wait a little longer to go. Then there are the internal washroom lights that come on when you close the latch.

Second, the toilets are not Indian-style, and shouldn't be used that way. Why? Because like everything else on the plane, they are made out of lightweight material that isn't designed for the weight of an entire human being. Don't rest your feet on them, just your naked bum.

Which brings us to the next point: wipe the seat down before you sit on it, for your own sake.

If you are a man, I'd strongly advise you to swallow your male pride and take a seat to do the small job. In the front washrooms, especially of the Boeing 737 and Airbus 320, the roof slopes upwards, putting you further away from the pot and increasing exponentially the chances of your tinkle being splattered all over the pot, the floor and even the walls. If you still insist on doing it all manly, you've got to wipe that mess with the paper towels provided and— trust me when I say this—you've got to be a contortionist in that confined space to get it all. Put your ego aside and sit – there's no one watching you.

If you've got your infant in to change a diaper, there's a nice table along the wall that comes down over the pot and gives you the needed space. Just remember, after you are done, there's a bin in the washroom where the used diaper has to go, preferably inside a disposal bag.

Once you are done with whatever it is you went to do, for god's sake, flush. There's no handle; instead, there's a small button that when pushed opens a vacuum valve which sucks the contents into an onboard septic tank. This mode of cleaning is actually much more hygienic and saves more water than the ones we use in our homes.

As you wash your hands, you'll notice on some aircraft that the water tends to accumulate in the basin. There's a plunger behind the tap to drain it out and takes a simple 5-second press to do so. After you're done, wipe down the wash basin with the paper towels provided, of which there are plenty. These used tissues go in a bin below the basin.

Finally, take a few seconds more to wipe the seat down with those generously provided paper towels before you exit the washroom.

Litterbug! In the course of a flight, there's a lot of waste that every passenger generates. There are paper cups, plates, bowls, tissues and these are just from the food service. From time to time the cabin crew make announcements requesting you to dispose your trash 'in the interest of on-time performance', then walk around with trash bags inviting you to drop all your waste into it. There's a good reason for it.

Have you seen that YouTube video "7-Minute Miracle"? It shows how at each stop of the famous Japanese Shinkansen 'Bullet' train, an army of cleaners walks into each compartment of the train and cleans it, fresh for the return journey, all within a tight timeline of seven minutes. One of the reasons why it takes so little time is because the Japanese – a culturally fastidious people – leave so little to clean up anyway.

The same applies on board an aircraft; if anything, the timelines are tighter. In the course of a 20-30 minute turnaround, passengers have to disembark and the cabin cleaned before incoming passengers are allowed to board. These are linear activities; one can't start before the previous has finished. By helping to clean up before you leave, you are actually helping the airline maintain on-time performance!

So the next time your flight is late, or you are standing in the bus interminably for no discernible reason while waiting to board, consider that it may just have been due to some casual passengers in the previous flight who couldn't be bothered to help with the clearance. Then make a mental note to yourself to do your bit once on board.

Stretching Your Legs. Sitting in one position can get tiring, and on long flights there is a risk of developing Deep Vein Thrombosis. So its only right that you need to stretch. Here too, there are a few things to consider before you get up.

Obviously you can't get up while the seat belt sign is on. It doesn't make much sense to walk around when the food service is in full swing either. Now if you're not in the aisle seat, you need to jump over the person who is, so keep your walkabouts to the minimum, preferably combining it with your washroom trip.

Travelling with Children. Internationally, the issues related to children on board aircraft have polarised air travellers like no other. A screaming baby in a pressurised metal tube seems to send the collective blood pressures of other passengers rising like a high-speed elevator in the Burj Khalifa. In online polls, a surprisingly large number of people have even suggested the implementation of adult-only flights. Since air travel is the dominant way of crisscrossing the globe, and since airlines have to look at their bottom line while filling up their planes, this is unlikely to happen, so it pays to tackle the problem with a cool head and cooler mind.

For parents with infants and toddlers who need to travel, there are a lot of ways you can make sure your baby is comfortable throughout the flight. Packing right is the first step, and at the very least, your baby bag should contain diapers, wet wipes, a change of clothes, a bib and a few soft toys to keep them busy. Since airport security globally does not permit you to carry liquid more than 100ml, you could instead carry enough bottles for the flight containing pre-measured powdered formula that can be filled with the hot water on board, which the cabin crew will gladly provide you.

Babies cry because they cannot talk yet, and this is their way of telling you that they are hot, cold, wet, hungry, sleepy or need to burp. They also cry if their ears do not adjust to changes in cabin pressure, which usually happens only if they have an ear infection. While adults with blocked nasal passages can resort to valsalva, babies need to swallow to pop their ears and there's no better way to get them to do that than to feed them or give them a pacifier. Ears pop easily during a climb, when cabin pressures reduce, but the Eustachian tubes do not respond so easily during a descent, so have a bottle ready soon after the Captain announces the impending arrival at the destination.

Another reason babies cry is because they are uncomfortable, and this usually occurs because many young parents select the cheap option of carrying infants in their arms. While this is legally acceptable, it is not recommended, since it does not really guarantee safety during a crash or unanticipated turbulence. A child seat – the same that you use in your car – can be carried on board. This will of course bump up your ticket cost from the 10% usually charged for infants to the 50% charge you pay for older children, but if you value your child's safety and your peace-of-mind, the extra cost is worth it. Do check with your airline first though regarding any regulations they may have for child car seats.

Older children tend to be more physically active, so it can be quite a job keeping them content in their seats for hours at end. It's a good idea to carry books and toys they have never seen before, and ration them one-by-one to last the course of the flight. And while many parents may bemoan the modern 'scourge' of electronic toys, they can work wonders to keep them occupied. Just make sure that they don't make those annoying electronic noises that can keep others' teeth on edge, or at least get a device that has an earphone jack.

Talk to kids in advance about the behaviour that is expected from them on board the flight. Kicking the seat back, shrieking and clambering over the seats should be on top of your list of taboo behaviour to talk to them about. Promise them a reward for good behaviour at the end of the flight, and keep reminding them of that reward when they stray and you should be good for the next many hours.

While cabin crew may gladly assist you in taking care of your child when they can, remember that the responsibility of keeping your child quiet is yours and yours alone and other passengers may not hesitate to tell you bluntly how they felt about your child's behaviour.

Now, for those without kids, its understandably hard to tolerate a crying baby, but there are a few ways you can alleviate your misery. In-ear phones are the best as the music drowns out a baby's screams quite effectively. As for the seat kicking, ignore it at first, as it may just stop. If it doesn't request their parents in a friendly manner to keep a check on their children. And finally, do give them the some leeway – it may be your own turn someday!

General Stuff. There are quite a few other things that are not acceptable on board a flight; Putting feet up in between the seats up front, or on the seat back in front of you, or on the table, or cutting your nails (yes, people do that!) are some examples. The list is endless. Simply put, if there's something you wouldn't do in front of your friends in your living room, you shouldn't be doing that on board a flight either.

Please be more understanding with a neighbour who's flying with a cold or cough – their discomfort is usually amplified in the thin, dry cabin air. If you have a cold or cough yourself, please show consideration for your fellow passengers by carrying adequate handkerchiefs and decongestants. Basic etiquette applies here: cover your mouth and turn away from others when you cough or sneeze.

Above all, remember that you are in very close proximity to complete strangers – the kind you'd usually be with near and dear ones. So cut them some slack.

And finally, please use deodorant.

CHAPTER VIII

Descent and Arrival

At some point in the flight you'll hear the engines wind down gently and the nose lower ever so little. This is the time that the aircraft begins its descent, and indicates that the landing will happen in about 30 minutes from now. Its usually preceded by a farewell PA from the cockpit giving you helpful weather information at the arrival airfield. The descent, or the PA—whichever comes first—is your cue to make your final trip to the washroom. Once you are back in your seat, you are essentially immobilised till the time you get up to exit the aircraft.

As the cabin crew prepare for landing, you'll hear the now-familiar PA asking you to put your seats upright and your tray table and window shades up. This is a good time to stow your stuff back in its bag and put the bag in the overhead locker. Ten minutes to arrival and you can expect the seatbelt and no electronic devices lights to illuminate as well. Like the takeoff, the landing is a relatively high-risk manoeuvre and these actions are required for your safety.

As the aircraft descends, you may feel pressure building up in your ears due to the increase in cabin pressure. If your ears don't pop on their own, there's quite a simple manoeuvre to do so: pinch your nose, close your mouth and blow out and the ears will pop. Repeat as often as required.

You may also notice sudden vibrations accompanied with a slight sinking feeling. That's quite normal; if you look out at the wing, you will notice that the spoilers have come up, usually in response to a request by the controller to speed up descent.

More vibrations are to be expected when the flaps are extended to slow the aircraft for a landing. By this time the spoilers would have been retracted, so one vibration substitutes the other. Lowering the landing gear not only increases the vibration level further, but the noise level too rises significantly.

That landing was hard!

Many landings are deliberately meant to be hard. If its raining, expect a firm landing, which is done to break the film of water over the runway. Now, you may find this hard to believe, but if the film is unbroken, the aircraft wheels could actually 'float' over it and the brakes would be completely ineffective. We call this aquaplaning, and try to avoid it at all costs.

If you are going to a small airfield in a big aircraft, say to Dimapur in an Airbus 320 or Agartala in a Boeing 737, the runway length is often limiting, so pilots like to put the aircraft down as soon as possible. This could result in a firm landing as well.

Some runways have upslopes at the touchdown point that can be tricky to judge. Result: a hard landing that catches even the pilot off guard. On some runways, the surface condition is so bad that no amount of smooth rounding off can prevent the aircraft from bouncing all over as soon as it touches down. Kolkata's runway 19L is one such example.

A hard landing could also be the result of gusty winds that lift the aircraft up just at the time of touchdown, forcing us to push the aircraft into the ground; too long a float and precious runway length gets eaten up fast.

It could be just the opposite: a gust of wind that slams the aircraft down when it is trying to cushion the landing.

On rare occasions, it could be a new First Officer or Captain who hasn't completely got the hand of the aircraft characteristics just yet. But we learn fast.

After the landing, the aircraft might brake quite harshly and you could be thrown forward in your seat. This is to be expected on short runways so be prepared.

Staying Seated

After landing, it takes a mere 3-5 minutes for the aircraft to reach its parking bay, and just 5-7 seconds after the aircraft to stop for the seatbelt signs to be switched off, yet it never fails to bemuse me how passengers want to jump out of their seats and grab their handbags as soon as the aircraft comes to a halt. It'll be at least another minute or more before the aerobridge or ladder is attached and deplaning can begin; deplaning itself takes just 4-5 minutes. Even then, the bus won't move until its full, so there's really no hurry to jackknife up and go running for the nearest exit.

On rare occasions, its possible that the aircraft will move some more after its initial halt, perhaps to reposition itself. Standing around in a moving aircraft is unsafe. My advice: stay seated and take your time: your check-in luggage will continue revolving on the carousel till you come and collect it!

Say Bye to the Crew

As you exit, the cabin crew—and perhaps even the Captain—is there to see you off and wish you farewell. It's common courtesy to respond in kind, rather than being glued to your cellphone. Courtesy is a two-way street – if you want some, you have to remember to give some in return. Lower that cellphone for a few seconds please. And if you felt the landing was smooth, please feel free to compliment the pilot!

The Exit

On a domestic arrival, its usually straight to the belt (US term: carousel) to pick up your check-in luggage, then off you go in your waiting car to whichever exotic destination it is you have to go to. Before you deplane, the cabin crew will announce the belt number your luggage will be delivered on. If you miss the number, don't worry: there will always be screens in the baggage collection area pointing to your belt.

Certain items, such as golf bags, surfboards, wheelchairs, bicycles, baby strollers and skis are not placed on the belt and may require being picked up at the customer service office. Check with your friendly airline representative at the carousel to find out where to get them.

On International arrivals, it usually takes a while longer. There's the inevitable queue at Immigration, then the carousel and duty-free before you pass through the Customs channels. There are two channels in customs – the green channel where you can pass through if you have nothing to declare, and the red channel.

Different countries have different customs requirements, and these are often very complex and very detailed, so it's a good idea to acquaint yourself on these regulations *before* you leave. Not knowing them is no excuse, and you could be slapped with a heavy customs fee, or told to leave your stuff behind because you didn't know it was taboo. The good news is that these regulations are widely available online, on sites such as http://www.iatatravelcentre.com and www.immihelp.com, so it should be easy to plan your purchases even before you step out of the country.

That wasn't so difficult was it? We hope you had a pleasant flight!

CHAPTER IX

Casual Conversation

These Tickets Are Crazy Expensive. The Airline is Ripping Us Off!

In 1986, I had to fly down to Delhi from Mumbai. A train journey was much more inexpensive but time was of the essence. The ticket cost was a grand 1186/- by Indian Airlines - the only carrier then available. If memory serves me well, the cost of petrol then was Rs 8/- per litre. Extrapolating on fuel prices alone, that ticket today should cost 11,000/- or so. However, a search I did recently for travel a month hence revealed that the going price for a Mumbai-Delhi air ticket was 3000/- or so, all inclusive. On the same day, a Mumbai-Delhi ticket on the Rajdhani cost 4710/- on First AC, 2840/- on second AC, and 2060/- on Third AC.

Or take car travel for instance. The same Mumbai-Delhi journey would cost you 9,000 rupees. Too expensive? Hop on to your motorbike and you'd be spending 2,800 rupees.

That's not all – in real terms, these ticket prices translated to a mere Rs 2.21 per km. If you compare prices internationally, that's a steal! A London-Edinburgh ticket on the same day by train was £120 – that's 17.35 rupees per km! The same journey by EasyJet was 5.78 per km, while by bus it was slightly cheaper at 4.62 per km.

Or take the US: a flight between Denver, CO to St Louis, MO – roughly the same distance as Mumbai to Delhi – costs $149, or about 9400/-.

Perhaps you've been the victim of 'preferential pricing'. You probably walked into the airport a few hours before the flight and found the prices going through the roof. Well, preferential pricing is now the norm across the board. Movie tickets, theatre seats or even hiring a motorbike is more expensive on weekends. Shopping for clothes or white goods, you've probably seen the reverse: if you want that fancy pair of Levis or Reeboks, you'd probably wait for that 70% off sale.

An airline ticket is no different.

Which Sector Do You Fly?

This is a question I get to hear a lot. The answer is, many of them. A 'sector' is a flight between two cities, say between Bangalore and Hyderabad. On any given day, I could fly four or five sectors, each of them to a different place. These are called 'patterns'. Depending upon where I'm based, I could fly multiple patterns to myriad destinations in the course of a month. So there's really no answer to that question. Which sector do I fly? Well, all of them.

Layovers Must Be Fun!

This myth harks back to another era, where the privileged few pilots flying long international sectors got to spend a week after every flight at an exotic foreign location before returning home. Today, when time is money, these layovers are much shorter. On domestic sectors, layovers can at times be less than 12 hours, just about giving the crew enough time to reach the hotel and catch a few hours of sleep before heading out again.

Often, a layover happens after the crew woke up at some ungodly hour in the morning to operate a four sector pattern. 12 hours later, as they get off the plane, they are quite bushed and the only thought in their minds is to hit the sack and get some well-needed rest. Come evening, and you're more likely to find the crew in the gym than on the beach – there's always an upcoming medical exam that keeps us on our toes.

Standard patterns often means that crew have layovers at the same place again and again. Hitting the Goa beaches on the first layover can be cool, but by the twentieth visit, Goa can start to become a drag. Ditto Kolkata, Guwahati, Jaipur, or any 'exotic' city where layovers usually happen.

What Does it Take to Become an Airline Pilot?

The path to becoming an airline pilot is long and arduous. It starts with basic flying training that take a year and involves a lot of studying. Subjects include aerodynamics, meteorology, navigation, radio aids, radio telephony, regulations, aircraft technical studies and aircraft performance. 60 hours of flying later, a student pilot earns a private pilot's licence (PPL). Another 140 hours, and its time to appear for the Commercial Pilot's Licence (CPL), in which the pilot takes written papers as well as flying a skill test. On the side, an aspiring pilot has to obtain a Flight Radio Operator's Telephony Licence to be able to communicate while in the air.

Having obtained the CPL, the pilot can now apply for commercial jobs. Big airlines are the most sought after, but there is also a buoyant market in the charter and private aircraft business. Entry tests for airlines are quite stringent and include knowledge tests, psychological testing and simulator skill tests. Once through, the pilot has to learn all about the new aircraft, both through books and simulator sessions, then go through extended on-the-job training and checks before being cleared to fly as a co-pilot.

The pilot then accumulates experience and can apply for the Airline Transport Pilot Licence after 1500 hours of flying. That licence once again includes advanced tests in the subjects I mentioned earlier and flying skills checks on the aircraft type, including checks on how to fly the aircraft completely 'blind' (known as the Instrument Rating). This by itself is usually not enough to earn Command of an aircraft as airlines usually insist on a minimum of 2,500 hours before they take up a First Officer for Command Training.

Command Training itself is an involved process – there are written exams, a Command interview and many simulator sessions before the pilot is released to fly under supervision of trainers before undergoing still more checks prior to release as a Captain.

It doesn't stop there. A Captain can now aspire to become a Line Training Captain or Check Pilot. Further up the ladder are Type Rating Instructors, Type Rating Examiners and Synthetic Flight Instructors. Progression is a part of a pilot's life.

All this requires intense amounts of study. Each of the subjects I mentioned earlier entails reading tens of thousands of pages. Aircraft documentation alone can run into thousands of pages. Then there are company policies to study and Standard Operating Procedures to learn. Study is a constant in a pilot's life. It would be safe to say that the amount of effort required to be a pilot would be the equivalent of studying for a doctorate.

Man, your job is glamorous!

Well... No. As airlines crew, we have no fixed working hours. There are days we get up at 3 AM for a 6AM departure and there are nights we sleep at 3 AM after a 1AM arrival. There are also nights that we don't sleep at all, while the passengers behind get fitful naps in the seats. But while most passengers endure these hardships once in a while, odd hours and broken circadian rhythms are the norm for us.

Thinking of a quiet getaway this weekend? Well, we really have no concept of what weekends are. Or holidays. I've flown five Diwalis and four New Years' Eves in a row. I've flown on Independence Day, Gandhi Jayanti and all the other holidays you can name. I've flown on my wife's birthday, my children's birthdays, our anniversary and even on my own birthday. And I'm not alone; all of us have made these sacrifices, all so that *you* can get somewhere on these days.

We study. A lot. Each flight involves reading 40-50 pages of documentation that have to be gone through in detail before we even step on board. We study the Company Standard Operating Procedures repeatedly to make sure they're hardwired into our brains. Documentation on each aircraft that we fly runs into thousands of pages that we have to read and re-read. Then there are domestic regulations and international regulations that we have to be aware about. All of it runs into hundreds of thousands of pages. We attend refresher classes every year. Once in three years, we practice how to survive a ditching, how to fight fires and how to jump off escape slides. We also have regular refreshers on dangerous goods regulations, aviation security and crew resource management.

My children see me studying much more than they do; both have decided that they never ever want to be pilots!

I sincerely hope they'll change their minds as they grow older.

We are the most examined profession in the world. Other than the annual refresher on technical subjects, we face two four-hour simulator sessions every six months where we are put through every conceivable situation that an aircraft could face in flight – engine fires, engine failures, system failures, near-collisions, windshear, microbursts, you name it. We also face two route checks a year to check whether we are following SOPs. We get examined medically twice a year. Something as minor as high BMI could set us out of the cockpit till we address it.

Yet, I get to put on a crisp uniform every morning as I go to work. I get to travel all other this vast country and see some interesting places. I have the best view out of my office window. And, I get to do a job that I love. I wouldn't trade it for anything else in the world.

You said the delay was due to fog this morning at Delhi. Seriously?!?

So you're taking the evening flight from Bangalore to Mumbai and its running late. As you settle down in your seat, contemplating the rush-hour traffic that you would have avoided had the flight been on time, the pilot comes up on the PA, wishes you well and breezily apologises for the delay, stating that 'the aircraft has been delayed due to fog this morning at Delhi'. Before your hackles are raised and you walk up to the cockpit to strangle him, consider that he may actually be telling the truth.

An aircraft makes money only if it is in the air. On the ground, its just a huge hunk of metal that costs money to park and maintain. Airlines schedule an aircraft to fly 12-14 hours a day. Turnarounds are restricted to the minimum possible, 30 minutes for medium jets, and perhaps as low as 20 minutes for the regional turboprops. A single delay on any of the myriad sectors it flew on in the day can have a cascading effect.

Now here's a little secret: if an aircraft flies at its maximum possible speed over a 2-hour flight as against its normal speed, it may perhaps gain 5-6 minutes at great fuel expense. In other words, its simply not worth it, so the crew don't really bother. What they attempt to do instead is ask for shortcuts, which are also of limited value, since most air routes are fairly straight anyway.

So, if a 7AM departure from Delhi was delayed to 10AM because of winter fog, its virtually impossible for the aircraft to make good on lost time, no matter how fast it flies. At best, an already-tight turnaround can be tightened further to save perhaps 5 minutes and the crew may be able to win back, say, 20-30 minutes over the course of a day.

If computers do all the flying, what do *you* do?

There's an old joke that goes: in the future, the cockpit will be manned by a pilot and a dog. The pilot's job will be to feed the dog, and the dog's job will be to bite the pilot if he tries to touch anything.

Cockpit automation has shot up by leaps and bounds in the last few decades, from the simple autopilots of yesteryears to sophisticated flight management computers of today. There's so much talk of automation nowadays that most people think that pilots have nothing to do at all, and are overpaid to sit and stare and the dials and controls doing their thing. Well, nothing could be further from the truth.

Automation in the cockpit has worked largely to reduce the workload and increase safety. Today's airspace is very crowded and flying an aircraft manually into busy terminal airspace such as Mumbai or Delhi would not only be extremely demanding but likely dangerous without the required degree of automation. Today's arrivals and departures demand lateral precision of less than 3 miles and vertical precision of *less than 150 feet*. It is very common for two aircraft to cross each other with a thousand feet of separation; if the two pilots were flying it manually beyond these safety limits, the risk of collision would be very strong indeed.

If you are old enough, you probably remember having to prime your Yezdi or Bullet with a few well-placed strokes as a prelude to starting a cold engine. Get it right, and the engine would tick at the first stroke. Get it wrong, and you could spend half a day trying to vent a flooded cylinder head. If you're older still, you probably have memories of hand-cranking that Morris Oxford. Today, it takes the push of the button for the engine to start. It's the same with aircraft engines. The start cycle of those massive turbines is controlled automatically by the Full Authority Digital Engine Controller (FADEC), which simply requires the pilot to move a lever from one position to another.

Or take a landing for example. As the aircraft touches down, the spoilers deploy and brakes are applied automatically. Doing this manually means that the resultant delay of a second or so could cause the aircraft to take a few hundred extra feet to come to a stop. Not a problem on a long runway such as Delhi, but definitely an issue on shorter runways such as Jammu and Agartala. Throw in a hot day and a planeful of passengers and suddenly the margins become very tight. That's where automation plays a role.

Have you ever planed over a fresh film of water in a car? I have, and the two of us in the car missed being run over by a truck by inches. In those days, cars didn't have modern safety features such as ABS and traction control; if they did, braking would have been completely uneventful. Aircraft brakes have antilock systems as well that permits them to land safely at nearly 300 kmph on waterlogged runways. That's automation at work too.

What do you do, besides pushing a pedal here and pressing a button there?

So what do the pilots actually do? We start by talking. As it turns out, we talk a lot – to one another, to the cabin crew, to the ground staff, the engineers, ground control, radar controllers, from one controller to another to yet another. This talking continues through the course of a flight, whether to obtain weather information, traffic information, taxi routes, departure runways, departure instructions, climb restrictions, position of other traffic, to speed or slow down, to climb or descend, to discuss between ourselves which way to deviate around that great big cumulonimbus towering above 60,000 feet ahead, to ask the controller for deviation around it, to get arrival information, to discuss how we're going to fly that arrival, to obtain landing clearance and finally to get taxi clearance after landing so that we don't bump into other great big airplanes loitering around.

We taxi the aircraft manually, both before take off and after landing, sometimes on one engine. We ensure we've copied the complicated taxi instructions and follow them accurately. Sample this instruction at Delhi: "taxi via Zulu Six, Charlie Whiskey Two, November, cross Runway One Zero, Kilo, Runway Zero Niner, Charlie One, Echo Two, Bravo Two to stand Two Five." And that's a simple one.

We do takeoffs manually. *All* takeoffs *all* over the world are done manually. That includes countering the effects of wind, keeping the aircraft nose pointed in the right direction, and while rotating for takeoff, making sure that our tail doesn't hit the ground.

After engaging the autopilot, we don't just sit back and have a cup of coffee. After all, the autopilot needs to be told what to do: which altitude to climb to, what speed to maintain, what direction to go in. We navigate the aircraft, make sure it is going where we want it to.

Throughout the climb, cruise and descent, we monitor engine instruments, flight parameters and the presence of other aircraft in the vicinity. We monitor the position of high ground nearby and our safety margins from it. We monitor weather and decide the most effective way of deviating around it. We monitor fuel consumption and take calls on whether to climb or descend to save more fuel. We ask for shortcuts that will save us even more fuel, then we execute those shortcuts through the autopilot. We monitor the destination weather to figure out whether we can actually land there or will have to go someplace else. We monitor the fuel closely to make sure that we depart for that 'someplace else' in the right time. Well before that, we determine whether that 'someplace else' is appropriate for us to divert to. Is it's runway long enough, hard enough and wide enough? Does it have ILS? Is the weather above minimums? Will it have jet fuel for us to tank up? Do we have company support there? Will the passengers be looked after at that place? All these are questions we ask ourselves before deciding which 'someplace else' its going to be.

We do the landings manually too. All except the ones where we don't have a choice. Pilots *hate* to hand over controls to the automation for the landing, but there are times, mainly in dense fog, where we cannot rely on our eyes to know where we are going and have to let the computers use their electronic eyes to decide. That allows us to get the plane down on the ground in near-zero visibility and for you to get home safely and in time.

Finally, and this is important: when the aircraft malfunctions, we use all that amassed knowledge and skills to figure out what, why, and how to get the aircraft down safely with the problem still persisting. After all, we can't just stop on the side of the road and call for a mechanic.

I Keep Reading of Drunk Pilots. Should I be Terrified?

The 'issue' of drunk pilots continues to get myriad column-inches in various media. The question is, did you actually fly with a drunk pilot on one of your numerous flights across the subcontinent?

Pilots and cabin crew are subjected to breathalyser tests before every pattern they fly. That's 2,500 breathalyser tests a day, or more than 9,00,000 tests each year. India is probably one of the very few countries globally that demands 100% compliance; in most nations, blood-alcohol testing is random. If that's not enough, the acceptable alcohol level in India is *zero*, and since our alcometers measure levels to the third decimal, a flight crew member with 0.001% alcohol in his bloodstream is officially considered 'drunk'. That's against the twenty-times-as-high 0.02% permitted by the United States' FAA and the globally acceptable 0.03% with which you can drive on Indian roads.

False positives can and do occur routinely at such low tolerance levels. Certain deodorants, over-the-counter cough medications and ketones produced by the body over long periods without food can trigger a positive breathalyser outcome. Recently, when our airline office was being painted, the doctor had to shift off-site as the paint fumes were resulting in a lot of false positives.

For flight crews, the consequences of failing a breathalyser test can be very serious. Caught once, and a crewmember can be suspended without pay for 3 months. Caught a second time, and the flying licence gets suspended for five years. Caught a third time, and you can kiss your flying career goodbye.

All that's fine, you say, but 33 crew members were *still* caught drunk last year. How safe was I? Well, all the testing was *before* the pilots even accepted their aircraft documentation for the day, so in the 1:25,000 chance that one of those was slated to fly you, rest assured he never got on the flight and was probably replaced by another (sober) crew member. The number of times you've flown with a drunk pilot in India is *zero*.

If both engines fail, will the aircraft fall out of the sky?

Have you ever seen a glider flying? It soars on the wind without any means of propulsion whatsoever. In fact, gliders have set some impressive aviation records, soaring to heights of 15.5 kms (50,000 feet) and covering distances greater than 800 kilometres.

Gliders are similar to modern airliners in one important aspect: they use the same principles of aerodynamics to fly. So when you're sitting in an aircraft, be assured that even in the extremely unlikely event of all its engines failing, it can continue to glide for impressive distances while the pilots work to restart the engines, or—if that doesn't happen—to land the aircraft safely.

On 24th June 1982, a British Airways Boeing 747 – then the world's largest commercial aircraft, lost power to all four engines as it passed through a volcanic ash cloud over Indonesia. It glided for 13 minutes, exited the ash cloud, and soon landed at Jakarta, 180 kilometres away, after restarting three engines.

On 23rd July 1983, an Air Canada Boeing 767 glided even further to a near-perfect landing from 41,000 feet after it ran out of fuel. None of the passengers were seriously injured, and all minor injuries happened on the ground as they jumped off the escape chutes.

On 24th August 2001, an Air Transat Airbus A330 flying over the Atlantic Ocean lost all power due to an undetected fuel leak and glided to a safe landing in the Azores. All but 16 of the 306 people on board walked off the aircraft without a scratch.

Here's an interesting fact: in each and every flight of a turbine engine, the descent for landing is essentially a glide; the residual thrust produced by the engines at idle is of very minor significance. This is a very effective fuel saving measure employed by all airlines around the world.

Isn't Flying Dangerous?

The short answer to that is, no. Flying is the safest mode of transportation today. The airline industry is highly sensitive to safety, and there's a ton of equipment, both in the air and on the ground, that is built in to mitigate the risk of accidents. ARSR, TCAS, GPWS and a whole lot of other four-letter acronyms work in perfect harmony to keep you safe at 850 kmph. Pilots themselves are highly trained professionals and go through regular, rigorous and gruelling training to keep it that way, while cabin crew go through equally rigorous training to save you in an eventuality.

If that isn't enough to convince you, here are some statistics that might help. In the year 2012, a mind-numbing 1.4 lakh Indians died on our roads. 29,000 died in rail accidents, of which 1800 were passengers on board trains. 23,000 died of causes attributable to nature, 27,000 due to drowning, 31,000 by poisoning, 29,000 died sudden deaths from heart attacks, epileptic fits, drinking and in childbirth and nearly 2,700 people died in structural collapses.

That year, 14 people died in air crashes, none of them in an airliner.

Safe flying, everyone!